TRACEY TURNER

STAT ATT

EXTREME
EARTH

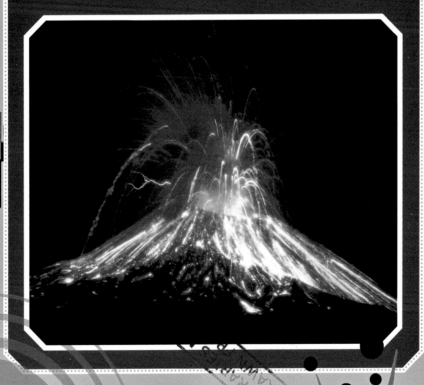

EDGE FRANKLIN WATTS

LONDON·SYDNEY

Franklin Watts
First published in Great Britain in 2015 by
The Watts Publishing Group

Copyright © Tracey Turner 2015

Credits
Series editor: Adrian Cole
Series designer: Matt Lilly
Art direction: Peter Scoulding
Photo acknowledgements:
Stephen Alvarez/Getty Images: 22, 24b. Arsgera/Shutterstock:
11cl. axily/Shutterstock: 29t. Anton Balazh/Shutterstock: 15t.
Eniko Balogh/Shutterstock: 25c. Benkrut/Dreamstime: 23.
Thomas Bethge/Shutterstock: 21cl. BMJ/Shutterstock: 29br.
Adam Bowers/Dreamtime: 1, 7bl. B747/Shutterstock: 21b.
Leonello Calvetti/Stocktrek/Getty Images: 4. CanadaStock/
Shutterstock: 7tr. dedmazay/Shutterstock: front cover tl.
f11photo/Shutterstock: 13. hanging pixels/Shutterstock: 24c.
harvepino with Nasa elements/Shutterstock: 20t. Stefanina
Hill/Shutterstock: front cover br. Hulton Deutsch/Corbis: 6tr.
© Ifremer / Dugornay: 17c. Jezper/Shutterstock: 19tr. Jarit
Jlrarativaro/Shutterstock: 5. kavram/Shutterstock: 14br.
Delmas Lehman/Shutterstock: front cover bc. Gavin Maxwell/
Nature P L: 17b. 1tomm/Shutterstock: 8c. Carsten Peter/
Speleoresearch &Films/Getty Images: 24t. Dmitry Pichugin/
Shutterstock: 25br. Patrick Poendl/Shutterstock: 11c. Daniel J
Rao/Shutterstock: 26b. Armin Rose/Shutterstock: 25t. saume/
Shutterstock: 25bc. sekar B/Shutterstock: front cover bl, 8t.
Guo Jian She/Red Ink/Corbis: 6tl. Todd Shoemake/
Shutterstock: 20b. TW Photo/Corbis: 10c. Pavel Vakhrushev/
Shutterstock: 11cr. Lee Prince/Shutterstock: 26r. Nickolay
Vinokurov/Shutterstock: 15b. Krysztof Wiktor/Shutterstock:
14tl. Andrea Wilmot/Shutterstock: 25bl. ZafiSF@Panoraamio:
26l. Alexandr Zhittsov/Shutterstock: 29bl.

Dewey number 550
HB ISBN 978 1 4451 4164 0
Library ebook ISBN 978 1 4451 2764 4

Printed in China

MIX
Paper from
responsible sources
FSC® C104740
www.fsc.org

Franklin Watts
An imprint of
Hachette Children's Group
Part of The Watts Publishing Group
Carmelite House
50 Victoria Embankment
London EC4Y 0DZ

An Hachette UK Company
www.hachette.co.uk

www.franklinwatts.co.uk

CONTENTS

Introduction

Did you just hear a sort of creaky groaning noise?
That's because this book is bursting with information about planet Earth at its most amazing, terrifying, explosive and perilous. In it you'll discover essential facts about volcanoes, tsunamis and hurricanes, the highest peaks and the deepest oceans. Quake with terror as you discover a jumping spider that lives higher than any other animal, and a hot spring that gushes spumes of superhot water every five minutes. **Find out about a town where it rains fish every year!**

As well as facts and stats, there are quizzes to test your extreme Earth knowledge. In fact, let's have one now. Before you start reading the book, see if you can answer these questions:

1) Where is the hottest place on Earth?

2) Which is the world's tallest mountain?

3) Where is the longest river in the world?

Read on to find out if you're right.

Prepare to stuff your brain with hundreds of amazing facts and statistics until it's ready to explode! (Actually, we should point out here that the publishers take no responsibility whatsoever for exploding brains.)

Planet Earth's Vital Statistics

Planet Earth has been spinning through space for the last 6 billion years or so, and during that time it's changed a lot. The rock that makes up the Earth's crust has been busily splitting apart and rearranging itself, because it's made up of huge great chunks (called tectonic plates).

Many millions of years ago the chunks formed an enormous supercontinent, but then they slowly drifted apart. Even now they are moving right under your feet. In millions of years' time the continents will look completely different.

The Earth continues to reshape in other ways, too. Ice ages have sent great rivers of ice to gouge chunks out of the landscape, and the Earth's atmosphere has warmed up and cooled down again.

STAT ATTACK!

Planet Earth surface area: 510 million square km

Land surface area: 149 million square km (about 30 per cent)

Water surface area: 361 million square km (about 70 per cent)

Percentage of salt water: 97 per cent

Percentage of fresh water: 3 per cent

Highest peak: 8,848 m

Deepest ocean: 10,994 m

Top seven natural disasters that have killed most people

The natural world is capable of some extraordinary events, such as splitting apart into cavernous cracks, or forming crashing walls of water 30 m tall. But when humans get in the way, these natural events quickly become natural disasters.

YANGTSE AND HUAI RIVER FLOODS, CHINA

In 1931, raging storms and heavy rain caused the Yangtze and Huai rivers to flood. The water flooded Nanjing, the capital city at the time, and people drowned or were killed by diseases carried in the water.

Death toll: Up to 4 million

YELLOW RIVER FLOOD, CHINA

In 1887, the Yellow River (or Huang He) flooded, inundating around 130,000 square km of northern China. After the flood, around 2 million people had lost their homes.

Death toll: Up to 1 million

BHOLA CYCLONE, EAST PAKISTAN

In 1970, a terrible cyclone – the deadliest ever recorded – rampaged through East Pakistan (today it's the country of Bangladesh) and part of India.

Death toll: between 300,000 and 1 million

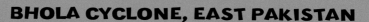

SHAANXI EARTHQUAKE, CHINA

In 1556, the world's deadliest earthquake shook northern China. Although it wasn't the most powerful earthquake recorded (it measured 8.0 on the Richter scale), it killed a lot of people because it affected three cities: Huaxian, Weinan and Huayin. The quake toppled buildings, caused landslides and opened giant cracks in the ground.

Death toll: Up to 850,000

TANGSHAN EARTHQUAKE, CHINA

The largest earthquake of the 20th century also happened in northern China. In 1976, the earthquake struck near the city of Tangshan and measured 7.8 on the Richter scale. It was so deadly because there was a 7.1 aftershock hours later.

☠ **Death toll: Up to 650,000**

CORINGA CYCLONE, INDIA

In 1839, a devastating cyclone hit the town of Coringa in Andhra Pradesh, in eastern India.

☠ **Death toll: Up to 300,000**

TSUNAMI, INDIAN OCEAN

The tsunami in 2004 was the largest ever recorded and affected 14 Asian countries (the worst hit was Indonesia). It was triggered by an earthquake on the ocean floor – the third largest ever recorded.

☠ **Death toll: around 250,000**

TALLEST TSUNAMI

The Indian Ocean tsunami of 2004 was the deadliest, but not the tallest. In 1958 in Alaska, an earthquake made tonnes of rock fall into a narrow inlet, which in turn caused the biggest wave ever recorded. The huge wave was 70 m higher than the Empire State Building!

Height of tallest tsunami: 520 m

Four Especially Violent Volcanoes

Volcanoes form where boiling, liquid rock builds up under the Earth's crust, ready to come shooting out at weak spots above. Since volcanoes can spew massive red-hot rivers of lava, they're also responsible for some of the world's worst natural disasters.

Mount Tambora

Mount Tambora in Indonesia erupted in 1815. It was the biggest volcanic eruption ever recorded and could be heard on the island of Sumatra, 2,000 km away. Tens of thousands of people died. Ash from the volcano blocked the Sun's rays and affected the weather all over the world.

 Mount Vesuvius

In 79 CE, an eruption of Mount Vesuvius in Italy covered the Roman cities of Pompeii and Herculaneum in choking ash and gas, killing thousands of people. It's one of the most infamous volcanic eruptions ever, and there have been more than 30 eruptions since then. Vesuvius is considered the most dangerous volcano in the world because it's only 9 km from the city of Naples, where 3 million people live.

Krakatoa

In 1883, the eruption of Krakatoa in Indonesia could be heard thousands of kilometres away. The eruption also caused tsunamis, and killed more than 36,000 people. Krakatoa erupted so violently that the whole mountain was destroyed.

Mount St Helens

In 1980, Mount St Helens in Washington State, USA, literally blew its top. The volcano ended up nearly 400 m shorter than before the eruption!

Volcanic Quiz

1
Hot, liquid rock that shoots out of a volcano is called...

A) Obsidian

B) Lava

C) Jet

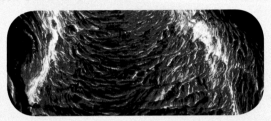

2
Which is considered the most dangerous volcano in the world?

A) Vesuvius   B) Krakatoa   C) Tambora

3
Which of these volcanoes blew its top in 1980?

A) Tambora

B) St Helens

C) Krakatoa

4
Which of these Roman cities was destroyed by Vesuvius in 79 CE?

A) Londinium   B) Aquincum   C) Pompeii

5
Which volcano erupted in 1883, setting off deadly tsunamis?

A) Stromboli   B) Krakatoa   C) Fuji

Explosive answers **on page 30**

Extreme Earthquakes

Earthquakes happen when the huge plates that make up the Earth's crust push against each other and sometimes slip or move suddenly. The two most deadly earthquakes to date both happened in China – the Shaanxi earthquake and the Tangshan earthquake (on pages 6–7). Earthquakes are measured using the Richter scale, which assigns a number to the amount of energy released – quakes with a Richter score of four or below don't usually cause much damage.

Here are some of the world's biggest quakes.

VALDIVIA, CHILE 1960

STAT ATTACK!

The strongest earthquake EVER recorded!

Death toll: 1,655

Richter scale: 9.5

PRINCE WILLIAM SOUND, ALASKA 1964

STAT ATTACK!

Death toll: 128

Richter scale: 9.2

SENDAI, JAPAN 2011

The earthquake caused a massive tsunami that caused even more damage and loss of life.

STAT ATTACK!

Death toll: Around 16,000

Richter scale: 9.0

KAMCHATKA, RUSSIA 1952

STAT ATTACK!

Despite its high score on the Richter scale, no lives were lost as a result of this earthquake – though a farmer in Hawaii reported the death of six cows because of the tsunami the earthquake caused.

Death toll: 0

Richter scale: 9.0

KOBE, JAPAN 1995

STAT ATTACK!

In addition to the people killed, this earthquake destroyed over 45,000 homes and injured 30,000 people.

Death toll: Over 6,000

Richter scale: 7.2

BAM, IRAN 2003

STAT ATTACK!

This earthquake destroyed more than 70 per cent of the city of Bam's buildings. Even though it's the least powerful on our list, it killed the most people.

Death toll: Around 30,000

Richter scale: 6.6

STAT ATTACK!

NAME
Mauna Kea

HEIGHT
10,205 m

LOCATION
Hawaii

You thought this was going to be Mount Everest, didn't you? Well, it's not! Notice that this is the world's **'tallest'** mountain, not the world's **'highest'**. That's because most of this mountain is under the sea – 4,205 m of it rises above the surface, but its underwater base is much further down. **Altogether it's 1,357 m taller than Mount Everest.**

The World's Five **Highest** Peaks

The Himalayas are the tallest mountains in the world. All five of the world's highest peaks are in the Himalaya mountain range...

1

2

3

STAT ATTACK!

NAME
Mount Everest

HEIGHT
8,848 m

LOCATION
China & Nepal

NAME
K2

HEIGHT
8,611 m

LOCATION
China & Pakistan

NAME
Kangchenjunga

HEIGHT
8,586 m

LOCATION
India & Nepal

	NAME	HEIGHT	LOCATION
4	Lhotse	8,516 m	China & Nepal
5	Makalu	8,463 m	China & Nepal

Highest Mountains of the Seven Continents

It does seem a bit unfair that all five of the tallest mountains in the world are in the Himalayas.

Here are the highest peaks on all seven continents:

NAME
Mount Everest

CONTINENT
Asia

HEIGHT
8,848 m

LOCATION
China & Nepal

NAME
Aconcagua

CONTINENT
South America

HEIGHT
6,960 m

LOCATION
Argentina

NAME
Mount McKinley

CONTINENT
North America

HEIGHT
6,194 m

LOCATION
Alaska

NAME
Mount Kilimanjaro

CONTINENT
Africa

HEIGHT
5,895 m

LOCATION
Tanzania

NAME
Mount Elbrus

CONTINENT
Europe

HEIGHT
5,642 m

LOCATION
Russia

NAME
Vinson Massif

CONTINENT
Antarctica

HEIGHT
4,897 m

LOCATION
Ellsworth Mtns

NAME
Kosciuszko

CONTINENT
Australasia

HEIGHT
2,228 m

LOCATION
New South Wales

In some places, deep in the earth, volcanic activity heats up water that's collected inside cracks in the rock. The heated water bubbles up to the surface to form hot springs. But some hot springs aren't content with just being hot and bubbly – they have to erupt in giant spumes of hot water called geysers!

There are about **1,000 geysers** around the world, in the United States, Russia, Chile, New Zealand and Iceland. Yellowstone National Park in the USA has far more than its fair share – about half. Here are some of the world's most gushing geysers.

1. Old Faithful

Old Faithful is probably the most famous geyser in the world. It got its name because it can be relied on to erupt in a torrent of boiling water at regular intervals. Now the average interval is about 90 minutes, but when Old Faithful was first named the intervals lasted about 65 minutes.

STAT ATTACK!

Where: Yellowstone National Park, USA

Height: Up to 55 m

Erupts every: 90 minutes (on average)

Duration: between 1.5 and 5 minutes

2. Steamboat Geyser

Steamboat Geyser isn't nearly as reliable as Old Faithful: sometimes it doesn't erupt for years – for example, between 1911 and 1961, and from 2005 to 2013 – then it might erupt three or four times in one year. On the other hand, it's more spectacular – in fact it's the tallest active geyser in the world. Its biggest eruptions can last 40 minutes, and when it's finished it puffs out huge jets of steam, just to show off, for up to two days.

STAT ATTACK!

Where: Yellowstone National Park, USA

Height: Up to 90 m

Erupts every: Completely unpredictable

Duration: Up to 40 minutes

3. Strokkur

Strokkur, which means 'churn' in Icelandic, erupts so often that you've barely time to eat your packed lunch before it's off again. It's one of two famous geysers in the Haukadalur area of Iceland – the other one is called Geysir, and it's the reason geysers got their name.

STAT ATTACK!

Where: South-west Iceland

Height: Up to 40 m (usually between 15 and 20 m)

Erupts every: 4 to 8 minutes

Duration: A few seconds (sometimes there can be a few quick eruptions one after the other)

WATERY QUIZ!

Use the Internet to help research the answers to these questions.

1

The Caspian Sea **is...**

a) The most salty sea on Earth

b) The world's biggest lake

c) The source of the River Nile

2

Which is the world's longest river**?**

a) The Amazon   **b)** The Nile   **c)** The Yangtze

3

The Great Lakes **of North America were formed by...**

a) Glaciers   **b)** Earthquakes   **c)** Volcanoes

4

The Dead Sea **is famous for...**

a) Treacherous reefs

b) Terrible storms

c) Being very salty

Splashing answers **on page 30**

THE DEEPEST PART
OF THE OCEAN

HOW DEEP IS THE SEA?

Well, obviously it varies quite a lot – some of it is shallow enough to paddle in, while some of it is deep enough for giant squid and blue whales and things to lurk in. On average, the sea is about **4 km deep**, but the deepest part of the ocean is more than twice that . . .

THE MARIANA TRENCH

The **Mariana Trench** is a deep gash in the sea bed in the Pacific Ocean, east of the Philippines and roughly 200 km from the Mariana Islands.

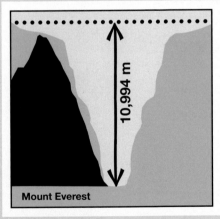

10,994 m

Mount Everest

Its deepest point is **Challenger Deep**, and it's called 'Deep' for a reason: it is not shallow. In fact, if you dropped Mount Everest into it, there would be 1.6 km of clear water above the mountain's peak. At that depth, nearly 11 km down, the pressure is fierce – you would be squished because the force of the water pressure is around 1,000 times higher than at sea level.

 Only three people have ever explored Challenger Deep:

✳ 1960 – Jacques Piccard & Don Walsh

✳ 2012 – James Cameron

STAT ATTACK!

Where: Western Pacific Ocean	
Depth: 10,994 m	
Length: 2,550 km	
Width: 69 km (on average)	

SIX INCREDIBLE
Extremophiles

You might think that absolutely nothing could live at the bottom of the **Mariana Trench** – there's no light, it's very cold (in most places), and the pressure is squishingly extreme.

BUT YOU'D BE WRONG.

Animals that live and thrive in Earth's extreme environments are the toughest on the planet, and are known as extremophiles . . .

1 Pompeii worms

Deep under the sea, vents spew a super-hot mixture of chemicals into the ocean. It's also dark and the pressure is intense. Pompeii worms survive inside tubes burrowed into the sides of the vents.

STAT ATTACK!
Extreme temperature:
80°C

Sahara desert ants

3

In the scorching heat of the midday Sun, Sahara desert ants pick their way quickly across the sand to grab dead insects to eat. The ant is one of the most heat-tolerant creatures in the world.

STAT ATTACK!
Sand surface temperature:
70°C

2 Himalayan jumping spider

STAT ATTACK!
Extreme height:
up to 6,700 m

This spider has a head for heights: it lives up to 6,700 m high in the Himalaya mountains, higher than any other animal (apart from tardigrades – see next page). It eats insects and other small creatures that get blown up to its lair.

4 Red flat bark beetles

Red flat bark beetles live in the freezing wastes of the Arctic. They stop their bodily fluids from freezing by producing anti-freeze chemicals.

STAT ATTACK!

Extreme temperature: **-100ºC**

5 Tardigrades

Tardigrades are microscopic water-dwelling animals, also known as water bears, and are the world's toughest animal. When they're fully grown most are only about half a millimetre long.

STAT ATTACK!

They can survive:

extreme temperatures

extreme pressure:
(more than six times the pressure of the Mariana Trench – see page 17)

radiation: (hundreds of times the dose that would kill a human being)

drought: (if there's no water, tardigrades can dehydrate and stay that way for YEARS, and then carry on as normal when conditions get damp again. No one knows how they do it.)

6 Bacteria

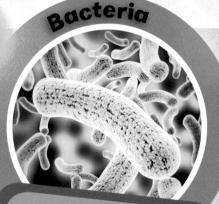

The hardest extremophiles of the lot are bacteria. They don't qualify as animals, because they're only single-celled. But they're tough, and they live and thrive in places where nothing else can.

STAT ATTACK!

They can survive:

extreme temperatures:
They can withstand even more extreme temperatures than tardigrades – in super-hot underwater vents and at the freezing cold Poles.

electricity:
Some bacteria live on electricity, unlike any other living thing on the planet.

HURRICANE
ESSENTIAL FACTS:

Winds up to: 300 km an hour

WHAT ARE THEY?
Large spiralling storms featuring heavy rain, strong winds and causing high waves.

WHERE DO THEY COME FROM?
Usually over large areas of warm water.

Also known as:
Cyclones in the Indian Ocean, typhoons in the Pacific Ocean. Hurricanes are sometimes called tropical cyclones.

TORNADO
ESSENTIAL FACTS:

Winds up to: 500 km an hour

WHAT ARE THEY?
A rapidly rotating column of air that touches the ground, featuring rain, hail and very strong winds.

WHERE DO THEY COME FROM?
Most common in areas of flat, dry land, especially in Tornado Alley, USA.

Also known as: Twisters

HIGH WIND QUIZ

How much do you know?

1 **Where in the USA are you most likely to encounter a** tornado**?**

a) A bowling alley   **b)** Valley   **b)** Tornado Alley

2 **Where do** hurricanes **form?**

a) Over warm seas   **b)** In the Arctic   **c)** Over the continent of North America

3 **What are** tornadoes **also known as?**

TORNADO

a) Whizzers   **b)** Shredders   **c)** Twisters

4 **Which of the following has the highest winds:**

a) Hurricane

b) Tornado

c) Tropical storm

Which cyclone **caused most deaths?**

5

a) Coringa, 1839   **b)** Bhola, 1970   **c)** Backerganj, 1876

Windy answers **on page 30**

FIVE
REALLY
REALLY
DEEP
CAVES

As far as anyone knows, the world's deepest cave is Krubera Cave in Georgia – though maybe someone brave and not afraid of dark, cold, damp, cramped spaces and creeping things will find an even deeper one in the future.

Good luck to them!

In the meantime, here are the **top five deepest caves** in the world...

1. KRUBERA CAVE

In the mountains of Georgia next to the shores of the Black Sea lies the only cave so far discovered that's deeper than 2,000 m.

Yes, it's more than 2 km down!

In 2007, intrepid diver Gennadiy Samokhin dived into a flooded tunnel (and don't forget this was already more than 1.5 km deep and completely pitch dark and uncharted) in the cave's depths to record the deepest extent of the cave reached so far.

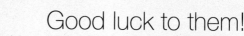

✳ **STAT ATTACK!** | **Where: Georgia** | **Depth: 2,197 m (plus or minus 20 m**

THE NEXT TWO DEEPEST CAVES ARE ALSO FOUND IN GEORGIA

2. SARMA CAVE

✳ **STAT ATTACK!** | **Where: Georgia** | **Depth: 1,830 m**

3. ILLYUZIA MEZHONNOGO-SNEZHNAYA

✳ **STAT ATTACK!** | **Where: Georgia** | **Depth: 1,753 m**

4. LAMPRECHTSOFEN

This cave system in Austria was walled up in 1701 to stop treasure hunters intent on searching for the legendary treasure of a knight from the time of the Crusades. In 1905, after the cave was reopened, human skeletons were found – probably what was left of some of the treasure hunters.

STAT ATTACK!

Where: Austria

Depth: 1,632 m

5. GOUFFRE MIROLDA

When it was first explored, this 1 km deep French cave was the deepest in the world. It no longer holds the record (Krubera Cave does), but we're still impressed!

STAT ATTACK!

Where: France

Depth: 1,733 m

TWO MORE IMPRESSIVE CAVES

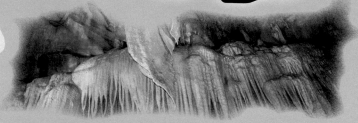

MAMMOTH CAVE IN KENTUCKY, USA.

It's the longest cave in the world by a very, very long way: at nearly 600 km long, it's more than twice the length of the next longest cave (which is an underwater cave system, *Sac Actun* in Mexico). It's longer than the distance between London and Glasgow! Imagine getting lost in there . . .

STAT ATTACK!   Where: USA   Length: 580 km

SARAWAK CHAMBER

The Sarawak Chamber in Malaysia is the biggest underground chamber in the world. You could lay One, World Trade Center across its length, the Eiffel Tower across its width (with plenty of room to spare), and stand the Statue of Liberty upright inside it!

STAT ATTACK!

Where: Malaysia

Length: 600 m

Width: 400 m

Height: 100 m

CREEPY CAVE QUIZ

Use the Internet to help research the answers to these questions.

1 **The** Naica Cave **in Mexico is also known as...**

a) The Cave of Doom, because it's full of treacherous, 100 m deep pits

b) The Cave of Crystals, because it's full of the biggest natural crystals in the world

c) The Bat Cave, because it's full of millions of bats

2 **What are** Snottites**?**

a) Cave-dwelling blind fish

b) Spiders that spin slimy webs inside caves

c) Slimy bacteria that hang from cave roofs

3 **What's the difference between the cave formations** stalactites **and** stalagmites**?**

a) Stalactites grow upwards from a cave floor, stalagmites grow downwards from a cave roof

b) Stalagmites grow upwards from a cave floor, stalactites grow downwards from a cave roof

c) Stalactites need light to grow, stalagmites don't

4 **What's unusual about the cave walls at** El Castillo **cave in northern Spain?**

a) They're full of tunnels that lead to a vast underground chamber

b) They're covered in sparkling natural crystals

c) They're painted with the world's oldest cave art

5 **What are** cave pearls, soda straws **and** moonmilk?

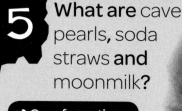

a) Cave formations

b) Creatures that live in caves

c) Semi-precious stones that are found in caves

Cavernous answers **on page 30**

Five **Dry** But Not Necessarily **Hot** Deserts

Not all deserts are hot.

In fact, one in particular is extremely cold. Here are the world's biggest deserts, some with lots of sand and oases, and some with cold, biting winds and even snow . . .

1 Antarctica

It might not fit in with everyone's idea of a desert, but Antarctica's very low rainfall makes it one. The lowest recorded temperature on Earth of -89° Celsius was recorded here.

STAT ATTACK!
Area: 14,000,000 square km

2 Sahara

The Sahara takes up a vast chunk of the northern part of Africa, and spans 11 countries. It's the world's largest hot desert. The highest recorded temperature of 57.8° Celsius was recorded in Libya in the Sahara Desert.

STAT ATTACK!
Area: 9,400,000 square km

3 Arabian

The Arabian Desert takes up most of the Arabian peninsula. Its climate is similar to the Sahara's.

STAT ATTACK!
Area: 2,300,000 square km

4 Gobi

Lying in northern China and southern Mongolia, the Gobi is a cold desert, and sometimes sees snow, but the temperature can soar to 38° Celsius.

STAT ATTACK!
Area: 1,300,000 square km

5 Kalahari

The dry wastes of the Kalahari desert stretch across southern Africa, through the countries of Botswana, Namibia and South Africa.

STAT ATTACK!
Area: 930,000 square km

Three Very Wet Places

After all those deserts you're probably ready for a bit of rain...

but maybe not <u>this</u> much.

PUERTO LOPEZ DE MICAY

MAWSYNRAM AND CHERRAPUNJI

MOUNT WAIALEALE

Moisture from the Pacific Ocean condenses over the Andes mountains and falls as rain on Puerto Lopez de Micay.

These two villages in the Khasi hills in the Indian state of Meghalaya are beautiful, but very damp indeed. In the monsoon season, between May and October, they receive almost all of their annual rainfall.

Mount Waialeale, on the island of Kaua'i on the Hawaiian islands, is a shield volcano and one of the wettest places on Earth. It rains there almost every day – between 335 and 360 days a year!

STAT ATTACK!

Where: Colombia
Average annual rainfall: **12,890 mm**

STAT ATTACK!

Where: India
Average annual rainfall: **11,870 mm (Mawsynram) 11,780 mm (Cherrapunji)**

STAT ATTACK!

Where: Hawaii
Average annual rainfall: **11,500 mm**

Ten Weird Rainfalls

You might think hailstones are bad enough, but what about being pelted with fish, frogs or worms?

For centuries, there have been reports of rainfalls of animals that have no right whatsoever to be falling from the sky.

There's a town in Honduras where it happens almost every year! The most common explanation is that the animals are sucked up by waterspouts (which are tornadoes passing over water), but it seems odd that the rains are only of one type of animal...

the weird weather remains a mystery.

1 Yoro, Honduras

Rainfalls of **sardines** are so regular here that there's an annual festival to celebrate the delivery of small, silvery fish from the sky. Rains of fish are the most common of animal rainfalls and have been reported just about all over the world.

2 Japan

In Japan, the month of June in 2009 saw various rains of **tadpoles** and **froglets**, and one downpour of small **carp**.

3 Rakozifalva, Hungary

In June 2010, the town of Rakoczifalva in Hungary was deluged with rainfalls of **frogs**.

4 Galashiels, Scotland

In 2011, pupils at a school in Galashiels, Scotland, had their game of football interrupted when it rained **earthworms**. Their teacher counted more than 100 of the slimy creatures, which had plummeted onto the football pitch.

5 Worcester, England

In 1881 in Worcester, England, there was a reported downpour of **periwinkles** – a type of shellfish. One of the shells contained a **hermit crab**.

6 Lajamanu, Australia

In Lajamanu, a remote desert town in Australia's Northern Territory, hundreds of fish fell from the sky in 2010. They were identified as **Spangled perch**. Fish had also fallen on the town in 1974 and 2004.

7 Odzaci, Serbia

The town of Odzaci in Serbia was rained on by tiny **frogs** in 2005.

8 Louisiana, USA

In 2007, there were reports of a downpour of **worms** in the town of Jennings in Louisiana, USA. Some of the worms fell in writhing clumps, and were still alive after they'd landed.

9 Salta, Argentina

In 2007 in Salta Province, Argentina, **spiders** rained from the sky.

10 Bath, England

In 1894 in Bath, England, there were reports that it rained **jellyfish**, or at least a gelatinous substance that might have been jellyfish.

The Coldest Temperature Ever Recorded

STAT ATTACK!

What: -89° Celsius

Where: Vostok Station, Antarctica

When: July 1983

Extremely Cold Pole Quiz

Planet Earth spins on an imaginary line called the axis.

At either end of the axis are the Poles, one in the north and one in the south, with the area around the North Pole known as the Arctic, and the area around the South Pole called the Antarctic.

N

S

Since the Poles don't get any direct sunlight at all during the winter months, they're pretty chilly.

But what else do you know about the Poles?

➡ True or False? ⬅

1. The average temperature at the South Pole is -20° Celsius.

2. Explorers first made it to the North and South Poles in the early 1900s.

3. Penguins are a polar bear's favourite food.

4. Antarctica is one of the driest places on Earth.

5. The Arctic and Antarctic are both continents.

6. There are no land mammals in Antarctica.

7. The highest mountain in Antarctica is higher than Mont Blanc, the tallest mountain in the Alps.

Chilly answers **on page 30**

Quiz Answers

Volcanic Quiz Answers (page 9)

1b) The hot liquid rock that shoots out of a volcano is called lava. Inside the volcano it is called magma.

2a) Vesuvius, Italy, is considered the most dangerous volcano in the world because it is so close to a highly populated city.

3b) St Helens (18 May 1980) – the deadliest volcanic event in the USA's history.

4c) Pompeii (near modern-day Naples, Italy) was destroyed.

5b) Krakatoa erupted in 1883, triggering some of the largest volcanic events in history. Two-thirds of the island were destroyed.

WATERY QUIZ ANSWERS (PAGE 16)

1b) There are arguments over whether the Caspian Sea is a lake or a sea, but most agree it's a lake, and the biggest one on Earth, with a surface area of 371,000 square km.

2a) and **b)** are in competition for being the longest rivers on Earth – no one can quite agree where they begin and end. They're between 6,400 km and 6,990 km long. The Yangtze River in China is the third longest at around 6,400 km long.

3a) The Great Lakes in the United States and Canada – Superior, Michigan, Huron, Erie and Ontario – were formed by a retreating glacier. They're huge, and between them account for more than half the world's freshwater by volume.

4c) The Dead Sea is actually the world's deepest lake. It's nearly ten times as salty as the ocean.

HIGH WIND QUIZ ANSWERS (PAGE 21)

1c) 'Tornado Alley' runs down the middle of the United States, through (mostly) Texas, Oklahoma, Kansas and Nebraska.

2a)

3c)

4b)

5b) The Bhola cyclone in 1970 was the deadliest ever recorded, and was one of the worst natural disasters. The consequences of the cyclone included a civil war – from which the country Bangladesh was formed!

CREEPY CAVE QUIZ ANSWERS (PAGE 24)

1b) Some of the crystals are 10 m long.

2c) The bacteria live in extremely acidic conditions, and have been found deep inside caves in Italy and Mexico.

3b

4c) The artwork on the cave walls is thought to be more than 40,000 years old, the oldest in the world.

5a) These formations are quite rare: cave pearls are balls of calcium salts; soda straws are hollow tubes, which can turn into stalactites; and moonmilk is a creamy substance made from tiny mineral crystals.

Extremely Cold Pole Quiz True or False? (page 29)

1) False. It's colder than that – around -50°C – but in the summer time it might average a nice warm -20°C or so. The coldest temperature on record was in Antarctica – a chilling -89° C (see below).

2) True. The North Pole was reached in 1909 by Robert Peary and his team*, and the South Pole in 1911 by Roald Amundsen and his team.

3) False. Penguins live in the Antarctic but not the Arctic, and polar bears only live in the Arctic.

4) True. It hardly ever rains in Antarctica – in fact it qualifies as a desert because of the lack of rainfall.

5) False. The Arctic is a sea surrounded by continents, while the Antarctic is a continent surrounded by sea.

6) True. It's just too cold! There are mammals in the sea, though – including seals, orcas and other whales, all of which are protected from the cold by a thick layer of blubber. People visit Antarctica to study it, but no one lives there permanently and no one ever has in the past.

7) True. The Vinson Massif is 90 m higher than Mont Blanc.

*Some people don't believe that Peary actually made it to the North Pole.

GLOSSARY

continents – The huge areas of land, also called landmasses, that make up the surface of the Earth.

dehydrate – Lose a large amount of water from a body or from a plant.

Earth's crust – The solid rocky upper layer of the Earth.

earthquake – When two tectonic plates slip or move suddenly, causing the ground to shake violently.

geyser – A violent hot spring which sends a stream of water up into the air at different intervals.

Ice age – A period of time when the climate was colder.

inundate – Another word for flood.

lair – A place where a wild animal lives.

lava – hot liquid, volcanic rock.

Richter scale – Method of measuring the energy released by an earthquake.

tectonic plates – The massive areas of rock that float on the mantle of the Earth. Each tectonic plate is made up of continental crust and oceanic crust.

tsunami – An unusually large sea wave caused by an earthquake or huge landslip.

uncharted – An area of land or sea that has not been mapped.

water pressure – The weight of water pressing on an object or living thing.

INDEX